the guide to owning a
Red-tailed Boa

rewnowski

Dedication

*This book was possible due to the
patience of both my husband Ken and my
good friend Erik Stoops. For all of their
time and love, I thank them dearly.*

T.F.H. Publications, Inc.
One TFH Plaza
Third and Union Avenues
Neptune City, NJ 07753

ISBN 0-7938-0275-X

This book has been published with the intent to provide accurate and authoritative information in regard to the subject matter within. While every precaution has been taken in preparation of this book, the author and publisher expressly disclaim responsibility for any errors, omissions, or adverse effects arising from the use or application of the information contained herein. The techniques and suggestions are used at the reader's discretion and are not to be considered a substitute for veterinary care. If you suspect a medical problem, consult your veterinarian.

www.tfhpublications.com

Contents

Boa Constrictors, whether they have red on the tail or not, are among the most attractive and common of pet snakes. A wide variety of sizes and color varieties is available.

Introducing Boa Constrictors

With more and more people looking for exotic pets, many are considering large snakes. Boa Constrictors, *Boa constrictor*, are among the most popular snake pets. They are easy to handle, very attractive, and readily available through pet stores. Boa Constrictors, often also called Red-tailed Boas in the pet trade, are desirable because they do not grow as large as some of the giant boids, such as Burmese Pythons, *Python molurus bivittatus*, Reticulated Pythons, *Python reticulatus*, and Green Anacondas, *Eunectes murinus*, all of which can grow to well over 15 feet.

If the new owner makes the necessary preparations to properly house and care for a Red-tailed Boa, a wonderful relationship will develop. Boas that are handled and cared for properly will bring years of pleasure to their owners and can live for 20 years or more.

Note that proper precautions should be taken when dealing with such exotic pets. The owner must use common sense and respect the nature of the animal. A happy owner is one who does what is needed to make their snake content. If you are ready to make the commitment, then a Red-tailed Boa Constrictor will do nicely for you—it is a wonderful snake and makes a great pet.

CLASSIFICATION AND BASIC NATURAL HISTORY

Reptiles first appeared on earth about 300 million years ago during the Carboniferous Period, but snakes did not appear until about 200 million years later during the Cretaceous Period, shortly before the end of the dinosaurs.

The study of reptiles and amphibians is called *herpetology*. This covers a very wide range of animals including frogs and toads, salamanders, snakes, lizards, turtles, and crocodilians. Many herpetologists (scientists who study reptiles and amphibians) specialize in a specific area, studying only snakes or lizards, etc.

All boas and pythons belong to the family Boidae. Boids have certain characteristics not found in other snake families, including the presence of vestigial hind limbs (visible externally as anal spurs) connected internally by ligaments, and the presence of functional left and right lungs (only one fully functional lung in most other snakes). In the wild, Boa Constrictors give birth to live young (meaning they are ovoviviparous), with 30 to 50 young common in an average litter. Boa Constrictors are native to Mexico, Central America, and South America.

This book will center on a snake known as the Boa Constrictor, known taxonomically also as *Boa constrictor* (which is quite odd—very few snakes have identical common and Latin names). They are very adaptable, being found in terrain varying from rocky semi-desert and scrubland to rain forest. Boa Constrictors range in tone from light to dark, with subspecies from the wetter southern parts of the range being darker than those from the drier northern regions. Boa Constrictors tend to have relatively pale brown heads marked with a wide dark brown stripe at the back of the head tapering to a fine line on top of the snout; there is another wide dark brown stripe behind each eye and a hatchet-shaped brown blotch in front of each eye. General coloration of a Boa Constrictor may be tan to brown with wide blotches (saddles) of different shades of dark brown to reddish brown. Many Boa Constrictors coming from northern South America tend to have the saddles on at least the tail centered with bright red; some of these Red-tailed Boas may even have reddish brown to pure red centers on the saddles over much of the back. The name "Red-tailed Boa" is due to this red tail coloration, which occurs in squares or diamonds. It is important to note here that "true" Red-tailed Boas are referred to the subspecies *Boa constrictor constrictor*, in spite of the fact that certain specimens of other subspecies may have tails that seem distinctly reddish (choice specimens of the Peruvian Boa, *B. c. ortoni*, for example, have highly reddish tails). Also, not all specimens of *Boa constrictor constrictor* will have bright red on the tail. Remember, a red tail on a Boa Constrictor is only a color variety and *does not* denote the animal as a valid taxon. Also remember that there are a lot of misinformed people out there who will try to sell *any* Boa Constrictor as a "red-tailed" Boa, so beware. Educate and protect yourself.

This beautiful *Boa constrictor constrictor* from Brazil displays the red tail saddles so sought by keepers and breeders.

The following is a list of *Boa constrictor* subspecies and the scientific and common names most often used in conjunction with them. Also covered are the range of the animals, plus their general appearance, and scutellation details. The views in this section are based largely on the collective evaluation of data both contemporary and historical and may or may not agree with the views of professional taxonomists. Hobbyists should be aware that even the herpetologists who deal with the taxonomy (identification and relationships) of Boa Constrictors do not agree on how many subspecies should be recognized in the species, how they should be characterized, and their exact ranges. All subspecies are variable by their very nature, and not every individual from even a single collecting area will agree in details of coloration and pattern. Individual Boa Constrictors without detailed locality information may be impossible to realistically assign to a subspecies.

AMARAL'S BOA

Boa constrictor amarali
(Stull, 1932)

A native of southeastern Bolivia and southern and southwestern Brazil. Ground color gray. Dorsal pattern mostly half rings or brown spots. Gray "braid pattern" on belly. Sides of belly and back (dorsum) covered with dark spotting. Scale counts: 71 to 79 dorsal

Peru also offers some beautiful Common Boas with strong markings and tendencies toward red tails.

rows; 226 to 237 ventrals; and 43 to 52 subcaudals. Average 22 saddles.

COMMON BOA

Boa constrictor constrictor
Linnaeus, 1758

Found over most of the northern and central sections of South America east of the Andes Mountains, including the islands of Trinidad and Tobago. Ground color varies, including browns, grays, pale pink, and reddish, with brown to dark brown dorsal saddles that usually are connected in a chain-like pattern. Belly usually is cream-colored with a peppering of tiny black spots. Tail saddles often mahogany red to a richer, brighter red, hence the occasional "Red-tailed" Boas. Scale counts: 75 to 95 dorsal rows; 227 to 250 ventrals; and 49 to 62 subcaudals. Average 15 to 21 saddles.

The following two subspecies are recognized by some herpetologists but not others, and their names appear in the literature on occasion. Neither form is widely available.

LONG-TAILED BOA

Boa constrictor longicauda
Price and Russo, 1991

Found in the Tumbes Province of northern Peru. Generally a very darkly colored snake with the typical Boa pattern. One outstanding feature is that the first third of the body is mostly gray, with the pattern marks on the head and sides being deep black, including a thick black mark in front of the eye. Scale counts: 60 to 76 dorsal rows; 243 to 247 ventrals; and 50 to 67 subcaudals. Average 19 to 21 saddles.

BLACK-BELLIED BOA
Boa constrictor melanogaster
Langhammer, 1983

Boas referred to this name can be found only on the eastern slope of the Andes mountains in Ecuador. It has a dark grayish ground color with a consistent black to brown, chain-like pattern. The belly, as one might guess from the common name, is black (often with light-colored flecks) even on juveniles. Old adults sometimes are uniformly dark. Scale counts: 86 to 94 dorsal rows; 237 to 252 ventrals; and 45 to 54 subcaudals. Average 20 to 21 saddles.

EMPEROR (MEXICAN) BOA
Boa constrictor imperator
(Daudin, 1803)

Native to northern Mexico through Central America, plus northwestern South America along the Pacific Coast south to Ecuador. At rarely over 8 feet in length, this is one of the smaller Boa Constrictors. The background color is generally very light but varies from locality to locality. The saddles are quite small and usually some shade of dark brown. It should be noted that, due to the immense variation in this subspecies, chances are there are a number of localized races

Many Emperor Boas have a distinctive head pattern featuring cross-bars between the eyes. Unfortunately, many of these easily found Boas have poor colors.

within this group. Some specimens appear very dark overall, while most have a lighter tone and greatly reduced saddling. The mysterious "Hog Island" Boa from islands off Honduras belongs to the *imperator* group and may be a distinct subspecies. Scale counts: 56 to 79 dorsal rows; 225 to 253 ventrals; and 47 to 65 subcaudals. Average 22 to 30 saddles.

Rarely recognized as distinct subspecies today, two names for island forms of the *imperator* group still appear in the literature on occasion. These are:

PEARL ISLAND BOA

Boa constrictor sabogae
(Barbour, 1906)

Native only to Saboga Island and the Pearl Islands in the Gulf of Panama. The indistinct saddles are set on a dark reddish-brown ground color. Scale counts: 65 to 67 dorsal rows; 214 to 247 ventrals; and 49 to 70 subcaudals. Average saddle count unknown. This animal is considered by some to be a color variety of *B. c. imperator*, but many others feel that it is probably isolated from the mainland. It has a strongly individual dorsal ground color.

TRES MARIAS ISLAND BOA

Boa constrictor sigma
(Smith, 1943)

Only found on the Tres Marias island group, approximately 60 miles off the Pacific coast of Mexico. This animal is

Specialists look for unusually patterned Boas, such as the small specimens that come from Hog Island off Central America. This may represent a distinctive local race of *Boa constrictor imperator*.

THE GUIDE TO OWNING A RED-TAILED BOA

The darkest of the Boa Constrictors is the Argentine subspecies, *Boa constrictor occidentalis*. These snakes also may have nasty dispositions and be hard to handle.

hard to distinguish visually, as the few known specimens are almost carbon copies of mainland *B. c. imperator*. However, the main difference is not so much in the snake's general appearance, but in the subtlety of scale counts: 77 dorsal rows; 253 to 260 ventrals; and 55 to 66 subcaudals. Average 35 saddles.

ARGENTINE BOA

Boa constrictor occidentalis
(Philippi, 1873)

This animal can be found in both Argentina and Paraguay. A generally very dark snake, the ground color being dark gray or charcoal, with the typical Boa patterning also being very dark, tending toward black with some light spotting. Many specimens are ashy gray with much speckling and a weakly defined row of saddles down the back, the head also darkly marked with indistinct stripes. Even the lighter phases of this snake are quite dark. Scale counts: 65 to 87 dorsal rows; 242 to 251 ventrals; and around 45 subcaudals. Average 22 to 30 saddles. Some herpetologists feel this may be a full species.

PERUVIAN BOA

Boa constrictor ortoni
Cope, 1877

Found only in northwestern Peru. Base color is a pale, sandy tan. Saddles are much darker (brownish to black) than many other Boas and can be connected either weakly or very strongly on the sides. Dark clouds often are seen between the saddles. Sometimes the head will have a pretty silvery blue/gray tinting. Some specimens may have a lot of red on the tail, making choice specimens viable "Red-tails." Some specimens are extremely attractive. Scale counts: 57 to 72 dorsal rows; 246 to 252 ventrals; and 46 to 59 subcaudals. Average 15 to 19 saddles.

Though formerly treated as subspecies of *Boa constrictor*, the following two Boas now are usually thought of as full species because they are widely separated from the major range of *Boa constrictor* and have strong characters of both pattern and scale counts. Neither is readily available in the terrarium market.

CLOUDED (DOMINICAN) BOA
Boa nebulosa
(Lazell, 1964)

Native only to the Lesser Antillean island of Dominica. Ground color is a dark brown on the first two-thirds of the body, changing to a darker and redder brown over the posterior third. Saddles on the first two-thirds of the body are a dirty brownish yellow, becoming a dark mahogany with black toward the tail. Scale counts: 59 to 69 dorsal rows; 258 to 273 ventrals. Average 32 to 35 saddles.

ST. LUCIA BOA
Boa orophias
(Linnaeus, 1758)

Native only to the Lesser Antillean island of St. Lucia. Dorsal ground color is a rich brown, with slightly

Boa constrictor ortoni tends toward gray tones but sometimes has a highly contrasting red tail, as in this specimen. This is one of the most expensive forms of Boa.

A young Peruvian Boa. Captive-bred specimens of this subspecies are eagerly sought and very marketable.

darker subrectangular saddles. Belly is white with speckling of gray or black. Scale counts: 65 to 75 dorsal rows; 258 to 288 ventrals. Average 25 to 31 saddles. Juveniles of this species are highly arboreal, some having been found in the wild over 30 feet above ground.

You might notice that the subspecies of *Boa constrictor* group into three broader complexes. Northern (Emperor) Boas tend to have more saddles over the back (22 or more) that are narrower than in southern (Common, Amaral's, Peruvian) Boas, which tend to have 15 to 22 saddles that often are relatively wide. Red tail saddles are characteristic of southern Boas rather than northern ones.

Argentine Boas, because of their dark coloration and high number of saddles, form a distinct group that is easily recognized.

Because of the technical problems involved in recognizing all these subspecies of Boa Constrictor, hobbyists should not dwell too much on the exact name to apply to any particular specimen. Many of the subspecies have been interbred in captivity, there are doubts as to the origins of many specimens in the hobby, and some dealers have a tendency to ask very large sums for "pure" specimens of the rarer subspecies or races. Choose a good-looking Boa with a nice personality and don't worry too much about subspecies.

A stunning Peruvian Boa, *Boa constrictor ortoni*. Your first purchase probably will not be of this expensive form.

Buying a Boa Constrictor

SELECTING A BOA CONSTRICTOR

When looking to purchase your Boa Constrictor, whether it is the red-tailed form or a more mundane but still beautiful specimen, ask if it was caught in the wild or captive-bred. Captive-bred Boas are preferable. They are less likely to be diseased and often are less aggressive. Also, captive-bred snakes are already acclimated to the confines of captivity. There are many pet shops that carry captive-bred specimens. If you cannot locate a captive-bred Boa Constrictor, your second choice should be a small wild-caught specimen. Wild neonates (newborns) to juveniles about 2 feet long have a good chance for being kept successfully. These will be easier to bring into a new environment as younger snakes are more adaptable and less likely to experience extreme stress.

It is important to have all snakes, particularly imports, checked for diseases and parasites before bringing them into contact with any other animals in your home. For this you should try to find a veterinarian who is experienced with snakes and willing to handle boas and similar species. Try the yellow pages for local vets and give each a call to see if any can take on the challenge or can direct you to a vet who will. Your pet shop may be able to give you the name of the veterinarian who takes care of their stock, while a check on the web may lead to someone who can help you locally. Because Boas are just as susceptible to diseases of all types as any other animals, it is always a good idea to have a vet who you know can handle any emergencies as well as a yearly checkup.

When purchasing your animal, be certain that the body has some good girth, i.e., no visible rib cage. There should not be a deep depression down the center of the back nor projecting vertebrae, both signs of malnutrition. There should be no obvious injuries, and the mouth should not have any mucous secretions or yellowish pus around the bases of the teeth. Make sure you feel the snake for good muscle tone. A Boa's tongue should flick at regular intervals with no bubbles appearing on the tongue or around the mouth or nostrils. If the tongue stays out too long or is not being flicked at regular intervals, the snake is probably not healthy. While you are holding it, feel for lumps. Check the eyes to make sure they are clear and that there are no parasites (mites, ticks) gathering around the edges. Check the vent to make sure there is no crusted material and that the anal scale lies flat against the body.

When buying young wild-caught Boas, be especially aware of the conditions under which they are being kept. Is their cage sufficiently warm and humid, with good lighting? If kept cool and dry (as in a simple aquarium cage in an air conditioned area), young Boas are especially susceptible to respiratory diseases. These often show up as bubbles on the nostrils, gaping mouths, and lethargy. It has been said that most wild-caught young Boas will suffer and die from respiratory diseases, with few surviving to adulthood. Buy only healthy snakes that have been kept in good conditions.

When checking an animal, be aware of its temperament. A snake that is captive-bred and handled on a regular basis usually will be more docile. If the only contact a snake has with its owner is watching a hand throw food into its cage, it will strike at that hand even if it is empty, so inquire about how often the snake is being handled before reaching in and getting your answer the hard way. Even a small Boa Constrictor has a large mouth, many pointed teeth, and a very small brain that acts on instinct.

It should be noted that the Emperor Boa Constrictor, *Boa constrictor imperator*, is the main subspecies sold at pet shops in the United States. Most specimens are from Nicaragua and other points of Central America south to northern Colombia. True Red-tailed Boas, with bright red in the saddles of the tail and sometimes the back, usually are imported from Guyana and Surinam in northern South America (subspecies *Boa constrictor constrictor*) and sometimes Peru (*Boa constrictor ortoni* and/or *B. c. constrictor*). Many Boa Constrictors are captive-bred in the U.S., and such specimens are, of course, more desirable for a first-time snake owner than those that have been taken from the

Most newborn Boa Constrictors, including the dark Argentine subspecies shown here, are under 18 inches in length, but they all grow quickly.

wild. The less expensive captive-breds usually represent Emperors, while the most expensive Red-tails tend to be Peruvian or exceptionally bright specimens with ancestors coming from Guyana or Surinam. Newborn Boas of any type sell for less than specimens over 4 or 5 feet long, as you might expect.

SIZE AND GROWTH

Newborn Boa Constrictors (neonates), are around 16 inches long. Adult size varies somewhat with the subspecies, but the usual maximum length for any Boa Constrictor is around 10 to 12 feet. Most Hog

Island Boas are quite small, rarely growing over 5 feet, and the largest of the group are the Common Boas, *Boa constrictor constrictor*. The longest Boa Constrictor is thought to have been about 15 feet long, but today few specimens over 14 feet are ever found. An old record of an 18-foot Boa Constrictor was reidentified as a Green Anaconda.

The growth rate of Boa Constrictors depends on the temperature at which the animal is maintained, size of the enclosure, and feeding amount and frequency. Snakes kept at cooler temperatures obviously will not grow as fast as those kept warm. Along similar lines, snakes that are fed less will not grow as fast as those that are fed more often.

HANDLING BOA CONSTRICTORS

The more a snake is handled, the more comfortable it will be with being handled. As stated earlier, captive-bred Boas usually make the best pets because they have been around people and are, more than likely, used to being handled. However, even "friendly" snakes will have times when they do not want to be held. If the snake coils tightly around an object in its cage, tries to hide, or hisses and strikes at you, it is probably not in the mood to be handled. Just leave it alone and try again another day. As pet owners, the reward for respecting and understanding your Boa will be a trusting snake that is more willing to interact with people.

When picking up a Boa, it is important that you provide the proper bodily support. Approach the snake with caution and gently pick it up with both hands, with one hand fairly close to the head. It is important that the snake does not sense fear in the handler, as many believe this will increase the chances of a keeper being bitten. Baby Boas can be held in one hand, with thumb on top of the head and the rest of the fingers curled underneath if the specimen is known to be a little nippy.

Specimens 3 to 6 feet long should be held with two hands by supporting the head with one hand and about two-thirds of the way down its body with the other. The animal will feel more comfortable if you let it hold on to you. Larger snakes should be held by two people or, at the very least, with another person present in case of emergencies. Constriction by a large Boa can render a person unconscious before the handler knows what is happening.

There are a few important considerations to follow when handling a large Boa:

*Always wash your hands before and after handling, especially if you have been handling rodents. A snake will not know the difference between a mouse and your hand that smells like a mouse, so you could be mistaken for food. The sense of smell is much stronger than the sense of sight in Boa Constrictors, and a moving object that smells like a mouse is, to the snake, a mouse.

*Snakes should not be allowed to wrap around a person's neck. The muscle movement from a snake's coils can constrict the blood vessels in people's necks and cause cardiac irregularities and decreased oxygen to the brain, thus causing unconsciousness.

*Larger snakes should be handled by two people or, at the very least, another person should be in the room

THE GUIDE TO OWNING A RED-TAILED BOA

so that if the snake starts constricting, the other person can help release the snake's hold.

*Do not handle a snake for at least 24 hours after feeding. This could harm it or cause it to regurgitate this meal.

*Do not handle a snake that has blue (cloudy) eyes due to fluid accumulating under the eyecaps. This "blue" condition usually precedes shedding by about two to five days. During this period sight is very diminished, to the point of being virtually blind, and the snake will be more prone to striking at objects entering its habitat.

*Don't get into bad habits that will cause the snake to strike at you. If, for example, the only time you open your snake's cage is when you are throwing in food, the animal will more than likely bite when you put your hand in to pick it up. Frequent handling also allows the snake owner to check the snake for parasites such as ticks and mites. By catching problems early, the chances of complete recovery are increased.

If the snake is aggressive and you still wish to handle it, some keepers suggest you place a towel over the snake before lifting. Once the snake is in your hands, it can be restrained by holding

Don't be misled by the calm demeanor of most Boas. All have numerous sharp, curved teeth and can inflict a bloody, painful bite. However, Boas are not nearly as nervous as most other large snakes.

BUYING A BOA CONSTRICTOR

the head behind its jaw with your thumb and forefinger. The body can then be held in your other hand.

Remember, Boa Constrictors in excess of 4 feet long can give deep bites. The injury is made worse when the handler's reflex is to pull away from the snake. A snake generally will bite only out of fear, the normal reaction being to strike and then let go. Although your normal response may be to drop the animal, DON'T. Hold on, then place the snake back into its cage and leave it alone. If the snake refuses to release its grip, it may be necessary to pull the head forward and push your hand in further to unhook the teeth. Remember, puncture wounds can easily become infected. For your safety, proper first aid practices should be observed, cleaning the wounds with alcohol and betadine and being aware of later infection.

TRANSPORT

Transporting can cause stress to snakes if not done properly. Short trips, such as to the vet, are best done by placing the snake in a cloth bag, clean box, or plastic container. NEVER PUT THE SNAKE IN A PLASTIC BAG! Remember to put air holes in all containers except cloth bags, which will allow airflow through the material. On particularly hot days, bring a spray bottle with you and mist the snake if you feel it is getting a lit-

tle too hot. Placing the bag or box inside an insulated cooler may help keep the temperature low.

If you cannot move a snake by car, you will have to ship it by air. This is because the U. S. Postal Service as well as United Parcel Service will not accept snakes of any type. Other carriers may or may not accept snakes, depending on size and local circumstances. Check before trying to ship a Boa Constrictor by any cheap and easy means—it probably is illegal.

Snakes shipped via air cargo should be placed in a cloth bag with strips of newspaper, then in a ventilated shipping container that is properly supported with newspaper or other cushioning material to prevent excessive shock. The shipping process should not take more than one day because long trips mean anxiety for the snake. Advise the shipper of the contents so the snake will not be left on a sidewalk or in the sun while it is waiting to be placed on the airplane. The sooner the snake is returned to its proper environment, the better.

QUARANTINE

Newly obtained animals should be quarantined until their good health is assured. Give them a chance to adapt to captivity and see if they will eat. A healthy animal will accept food and shed within the first month. Also, have a veterinarian check new animals for parasites and so forth.

An incredibly patterned Boa such as this striped red-tail needs to be displayed, but it also must be quarantined before being added to any collection. Be patient—you'll have the snake for many more years, so what are a few weeks at the beginning?

Because there are several airborne diseases that can be transmitted between boas and pythons, it is best to place all new arrivals in a room separate from any snakes you currently may be keeping. The quarantine cage should be simple and easy to clean, but it must provide the Boa with the proper heat and humidity as well as a secure hiding place. Decorations should be absent or kept to a minimum, and the substrate can be very simple, even just newspaper changed daily. Never use the same feeding implements for a quarantined snake as for an established snake, never try to refeed uneaten food to another snake, and always sanitize your hands before and after entering the quarantine area.

Suggested quarantine periods vary from two weeks to two months, but probably most keepers observe a newly obtained Boa Constrictor for two to four weeks before putting it with other specimens. This gives an opportunity to make sure the snake is feeding properly, assure that it has no mites or ticks, and give it a full veterinary examination. If the snake shows any signs of a problem (respiratory distress, trouble shedding, vomiting of meals), keep it quarantined and be sure you take it to a veterinarian.

Most Boas that are purchased are young specimens with plenty of growth ahead of them. If properly fed and housed, a Boa may live for 20 to 40 years.

RECORD KEEPING

Importance of a regular maintenance schedule for a Boa Constrictor cannot be emphasized enough, and records should be kept from the day the Boa Constrictor is brought home. Information on such events as purchase date, original size, shedding notes, feeding and cleaning dates, breeding, and illnesses should be kept. Keeping track of such data will prove useful later on. It is easy to forget such information, so don't rely on your memory. WRITE IT DOWN!

Notes often are kept on simple index cards taped to the snake's cage. Other keepers use small notebooks. Still others use one of the variety of record-keeping software now available just for this purpose. All these methods are adequate to keep a variety of notes, but some require more time than others. If you are stressed for time you probably will use an index card annotated each time you feed or the snake sheds. If you are a computer advocate, you might prefer to keep your notes on the computer, though this usually means writing the information down first on a card and then transferring it to the program at regular intervals. Just be sure you keep notes and file them so you can use the information to make keeping your next Boa Constrictors that much easier.

Keeping a Boa Constrictor

HOUSING

Before bringing a Boa Constrictor home, make sure you have the space to house the animal when it is fully grown. Your newborn snake will outgrow its 10-gallon home very quickly. Remember, a snake will not stop growing because its home is small (its growth may be slowed, but it will not stop growing altogether). Plan ahead to have plenty of room for the snake to be comfortable in and for you to be able to properly maintain it.

The room that will house the Boa should be completely "snake-proof," so in the event that it gets out, it will at least remain in that room. Also be sure the room has a lock on it; this is also a good way to keep children, visitors, or other pets away from the snake when you aren't around.

Cage Size

Although a 10-gallon tank might be fine for housing a baby Boa Constrictor, it will grow so quickly that a new home will be needed within six months. By the time the snake has reached adult size (just three to five years), a cage at least 4 feet long and 3 feet high will be needed to house it. Many keepers prefer to build their own cages, but this requires a bit of handyman skill, time, and patience. Fortunately, today large and quite adequate cages for Boa Constrictors and other large snakes are made commercially and sold in pet shops or are available through special order.

The best cages for larger Boa Constrictors are horizontal and relatively low. Boas are generally sluggish snakes that get their exercise when feeding—they do not need exceptionally large cages. As a rule, a Boa Constrictor can do well in a cage about half or less its body length (thus 4 to 6 feet for a Boa) and about 3 feet high and 3 feet wide. Some keepers prefer more vertical cages and give the Boa climbing branches. Because of the strength of a Boa, the cage must be well constructed and solid, so it cannot be forced apart. A wooden frame works fine, with a bottom of marine plywood that can take constant water spills. Three sides can be plywood or a similar material, with the front glass or acrylic and the cover of screening. Almost any combination can be used, as long as the snake is protected from drafts, there is not so much screening in the construction that it will persistently rub its snout raw, the cover can be locked, the snake is easily visible, and all the corners can be reached for regular cleaning.

As mentioned, commercially made cages are available for Boas or you can make your own. Many keepers modify an old cabinet or chest of drawers to hold a Boa. Commercial cages may be finished with waterproof plastic materials. An aquarium, even a very large one, is not really good for a Boa because it will be very heavy and hard to handle, while commercial cages often are fairly light and can be placed in many parts of the house unobtrusively.

Room Enclosures

Although Red-tailed Boas rarely will be so large as to require free run of an entire room, this can be done when keeping two or more snakes together. The room can be equipped with a tub for water (large enough for the snakes to crawl into), sturdy limbs for the snakes to climb on, and rocks to provide hiding spaces and help shedding. The door to the room should be spring-loaded so that it cannot be accidentally left open. The room should contain its own thermostat control so temperature can be properly maintained, and thermometers should be placed in the habitat so the temperature can be easily monitored. Some electronic thermometers come equipped with an alarm that goes off when the temperature drops below a designated setting. Basking sites also can be provided with the use of heating pads and basking lamps. For safety reasons, it is best to install a Dutch door or a double door of some type so the snake can be kept from making a sudden run through the door.

IMPORTANT NOTE: Very large Boa Constrictors (certainly over 8 feet) should *never* be allowed to roam freely, particularly where small children are present, because even the tamest Boas can be unpredictable in temperament. If a large specimen somehow got loose, there is the chance that it could attack and kill a child. Boas don't have the reputation for unpredictability as do many large

You can keep a newborn Boa in an aquarium tank for a few months, but you must plan for rapid growth and must have a larger cage available to make your Boa comfortable.

pythons, but a big Boa can be a dangerous snake. Most large Boa Constrictors are quite lethargic, however, but their bite can be vicious and they are strong constrictors.

Tank Security

Boas will explore every inch of their new home and are sure to find a way out if proper measures have not been taken. A rock, book, or board on top of the lid is not sufficient. A sliding or hinged door with a lock will be the best protection against escapes. Pets and children must be kept away from large Boas, thus the need for a locking cover. If using a room enclosure, cleaning is easier if there is an enclosed corner into which the Boa can be herded and then locked temporarily. A minimum of decorations makes cleaning easier and safer as well.

Positioning

Where you place the cage for your Boa is important. Because of the large size of the cage and the weight of an adult Boa Constrictor, it cannot be placed on a flimsy support. Many keepers put the cage on the floor, but some use strong aquarium stands or supports made from 2 x 4 lumber. The cage must be easily accessible for cleaning, so it cannot be placed too high to reach all the inside corners. It also cannot be placed in a window (direct sunlight will rapidly make it a deathtrap) or next to an air conditioner (cold drafts). A secluded corner out of major traffic is best; be sure that electrical plug-ins are available for the heat and lights.

A large Red-tailed Boa in a nice, simply decorated cage is a great conversation piece, but remember that Boas don't always want attention.

SUBSTRATES

Substrate (bedding, litter) should be of materials that are easy to work with. Paper towels, pine or aspen shavings, wood chips, bark mulch, and recycled newspaper all work well. Paper towels should be dry and uncolored so ink does not rub off on the snakes. (Newspaper often is used in a pinch, as it is cheap and absorbent, but it does have inks that can make a mess of things.)

Cedar shavings should not be used as they can be toxic to snakes. The volatile oils in cedar shavings can affect the lungs and cause skin blisters, plus it has been suggested that the oils can cause tumors. Though these claims are not necessarily backed by scientific studies, most keepers believe that their snakes do poorly on cedar, so it is best to avoid it.

Indoor-outdoor carpeting (Astroturf and similar types) with rubber back-

ing can also be used. It should be changed at least every two weeks, and can be cleaned by being vigorously sprayed with a hose and then dried in the sun. Keep it outside all day to remove odors and germs. Have two pieces of carpet cut to the correct size so that a replacement is available while the other is being cleaned.

Anything used for a substrate should be absorbent to help dry feces and urine before it becomes too smelly. It should be large enough to not adhere to food items and cause possible intestinal impactions. It also must be relatively inexpensive as it should be disposed of or at least taken out and thoroughly cleaned every 10 to 20 days. Sand and gravel are not absorbent and make poor bedding, as well as being heavy.

HEATING

Because snakes are cold-blooded, their cage should contain a heat source that brings the temperature to between 84 and 90°F. Place a thermometer on the floor of the cage or enclosure so that the temperature can be monitored. You might be better off using two thermometers, one near the preferred basking spot and the other about half way up the side of the cage. In this way you get a good idea of the temperature gradient inside the cage. Even if the basking area is 100°F or more, it is not good for the snake if the air temperature is just 70°F. A hot basking area cannot compensate for low air temperatures. Small, inexpensive electronic thermometers now are widely available and are better than old-style tubular thermometers. Most also measure relative humidity and have probes to allow readings from a distance. Some even record the maximum and minimum temperatures reached during the day.

Heat sources should be limited to one side of the cage to allow the snake the opportunity to cool down if it wishes, unless of course the surroundings of the cage drop below 80°F or so at night. In such a case, the area of the cage can be brought to a reasonable temperature by using a small portable electric heater. Remember, the air cannot become too cool or respiratory diseases will result.

Two types of heating are necessary for a cage. In the first type, the overall cage must be brought to a minimal acceptable temperature, at least 80°F. In the other, a rock or branch serving as a basking area is heated to an even higher temperature, at least 95°F, so the Boa can bask in warm surroundings. Both types of heating are essential to the health of your Boa.

For overall heating, you can use strips of electrical heat tape placed

Boas prefer simple housing conditions with few decorations. Because of their size, be sure that you can easily grasp the snake without having to dig it out first.

on the outside bottom of the habitat or large heating pads (pig blankets) placed under the substrate or under the tank. With both these methods there is little chance that the Boa Constrictor can be burned, as the heat source is outside the cage. If you use electrical heat tape, be sure you install it properly or have it put in by an electrician—heat tapes have caused major fires. Pig blankets can be bought at farm equipment stores and work well for very large cages. Of course, in some situations you can simply heat the entire room to the proper temperature (80 to 84°F) and not have to worry about supplemental overall heating. A small amount of daily variation in temperature (down to about 78°F at night) is allowable.

Basking areas usually are heated by incandescent bulbs fitted into conical hoods and placed on the cover of the cage, out of reach of the snake. The basking area and its lights usually are placed in one corner of the cage, which allows the far corner to always remain cooler, giving the Boa a gradient in which it can choose the proper temperature for its immediate needs. Incandescent bulbs become very hot (most keepers use 50 to 100 watt bulbs) and will severely burn any snake (or your hands) that comes into contact with them or their hoods. Basking lights must never be placed inside the cage or where the Boa can rub against them. A flat rock often is the best basking surface. Some Boa Constrictors will spend several hours a day basking, while others are comfortable with little basking. Basking lights usually are left on about 10 to 12 hours a day and are best controlled by heavy-duty timers. Because Boa Constrictors are largely nocturnal (active at night), they do not need special reptile basking lights, as they want mostly the heat without much interest in the wavelengths of the light.

Though they can be used as supplemental heat sources, hot rocks and similar items that provide high temperatures to the belly of the Boa are not recommended. A snake senses heat from above, so if it basks on a substrate with a concentrated source of heat, it may stay too long on the heat block and suffer severe burns. Pads under the cage are fine for general heating but are not suitable for a basking area.

LIGHTING

As for lighting, it has been said that some snakes do better in captivity if given full-spectrum lighting, lights that duplicate the wavelengths of natural sunlight. Special fluorescent light tubes are made to produce such full-spectrum lighting and can be purchased in pet stores that carry a good selection of reptile supplies. This is not to say a Boa Constrictor needs full-spectrum lighting, but it may benefit from it, especially if it is to be bred.

All the varieties of *Boa constrictor* (here a Hog Island form) need similar levels of humidity and temperature, and none like strong lighting.

As a rule, fluorescent lights are used in canopies with built-in starters. Simple shop light fixtures work well and are inexpensive. These usually are designed to hold 4-foot tubes, a standard size. If you choose to use fluorescent lights over your Boa Constrictor, you can spring for expensive full-spectrum lights or just use cheaper, common tubes such as natural or cool white. Fluorescent lights often are kept on for 12 hours a day and of course also must be mounted above the cage, out of reach of the snake. Though fluorescent lights are relatively cool, their plug-ins and ballasts can become quite hot and burn a snake that comes into contact.

The cage should never be kept in complete darkness, but normal room lighting or indirect sunlight from a nearby window is sufficient to give the Boa a sense of the changing seasons. If you choose to use fluorescent lights (in addition to incandescent basking lights—you must have the basking lights), experiment a bit and see how they affect your snake. Some specimens become more colorful under fluorescents, some become more aggressive. Each snake is an individual.

HIDEBOXES

A hidebox is an essential part of any

snake habitat, and Boa Constrictors will utilize them frequently. Some Boas have even been known to pull their food into their hideboxes so they can eat in privacy. The hidebox should be designed so that you will have access to your snake while still allowing it to feel secure. It should be large enough so the snake can curl up under it and rest in darkness, but it must also be small enough so the Boa can touch the sides with its back, which gives it a sense of security. Small to moderate Boa Constrictors will fit well into the ceramic hideboxes sold in pet shops, while they also will use the hollowed half-logs now widely sold. Large Boas may become used to basking and resting in the open, and it is hard to find a hidebox that will both accommodate their size and be light enough to move easily for cleaning. The hidebox must be sturdy enough to withstand the weight of the Boa moving across it at times.

ROCKS AND BRANCHES

Placing a rock and/or a branch in the enclosure provides a rough surface to aid in shedding. A further function of a branch is that it will allow a Boa Constrictor to climb, which it will do frequently. All wood products are particularly susceptible to filth and serve as hiding spots for mites, so they should be thrown out and replaced rather than cleaned. Mild regular cleanings can be performed with the aid of some sandpaper or by soaking the entire branch in bleach and then rinsing out all the bleach smell, but more thorough cleanings are not worth the great amount of effort required. Larger Red-tailed Boas are too heavy to climb much, but they will use rocks and hideboxes to help in the shed. Small Boas climb well and appreciate branches and other raised decorations.

WATER

A bowl filled with about an inch of water and large enough for the snake to enter fully should be placed in the tank. Make sure it cannot be over-turned (a heavy ceramic bowl or a steel bowl with a wide base should do the trick). For neonates or juveniles, make sure the water dish is not filled too high, because young snakes could drown; use a shallow bowl that contains only about half an inch of water. Large Boa Constrictors often like to soak in a child's swimming pool for an hour or two each day—the water helps support their bodies and makes the day more comfortable.

Almost all Boas will try to soak in their water bowls, which will become very dirty with feces and often with shed skins. They also will splash water from the bowl to the substrate. Keep the bowl and its vicinity clean at all times, even if it means changing it twice a day every day. The Boa should not spend too much time soaking as

A decent sized water bowl is needed for Boas to both drink and also to occasionally soak. Unfortunately, they have the habit of defecating in the water bowl as well, which means you must change it daily.

this could lead to skin blisters (bacterial infections); persistent soakers may have to have their water bowl removed most of each day.

CLEANING

The cage or enclosure should be thoroughly cleaned at least every two weeks. Fecal material left in a habitat for any length of time can be a breeding ground for bacteria, so check the habitat daily and remove any such material immediately with a spoon or cat litter scoop. Bacteria from our hands can be spread to the snake, so it is important to wash hands before, as well as after, the snake is handled. When cleaning the habitat, remove and disinfect the water bowl and decorations, and change the substrate material. A 10% solution of bleach is preferred for general cleaning. Make sure the habitat is thoroughly rinsed with clean water then dried before placing clean substrate material back in the enclosure. The water bowl should also be washed thoroughly before refilling.

Boa Constrictors (here *B. c. occidentalis*) are very efficient predators on small warm-blood-ed animals. This makes them easy to feed in the terrarium.

Feeding Boa Constrictors

When buying a Red-tailed Boa, it is wise to check on how it was being fed. Some snakes can be very choosy about what they eat, so new snake owners can be spared much distress if they learn about and follow their pet's established feeding regimen.

FEEDING IN GENERAL

Providing proper nutrition for your Boa is very important. Its growth rate will depend greatly on what and how often it is fed. For a healthier snake, it is better to offer several small items rather than one large one. If a snake is fed prey that is too large, there is a good chance the item will be regurgitated. As a rule, try to feed animals that are not much longer than two or three times the width of the Boa's head, especially when feeding juveniles. Frequency of feeding depends upon an individual's metabolism, but as a rule juveniles are fed more frequently than older snakes. Commonly a baby Boa Constrictor is fed twice a week, larger subadults are fed once a week, and full adults are fed every week to three weeks depending on how they react to the food. A Boa should be at least somewhat hungry when it is fed, so it will show an active interest in the prey. How much to feed can only be answered by watching the snake. One week your Boa might eat one rat, and the next week it'll eat three.

Never feed so often that the snake becomes overweight (obviously fat) or so rarely that it becomes emaciated (loose skin, groove down the center of the back, ribs visible). It is important not to overfeed a Boa. Overfeeding will lead to regurgitation, obesity, and possibly even death. One indication that the snake is hungry is increased activity. It usually becomes very active when hungry and seems to "search" its habitat for food, but just because a Boa seems willing to eat ten rats doesn't mean you should give it that many.

Boas Constrictors are, as their name implies, constrictors in every sense of the word and kill their prey by suffocation, an action often mistakenly described simply as "squeezing." In reality, a Boa Constrictor bites its prey to hold it and maneuver it into position. It then quickly wraps itself around the animal, and every time the prey animal exhales, the snake tightens its grip, thereby denying the animal the opportunity to take a breath. Eventually the prey suffocates; the prey is not crushed, though a few bones (ribs, limb bones) may be broken in the process. Then the Boa grasps the animal's nose and begins swallowing, head-first. Boa Constrictors and other snakes do not tear apart or chew their prey (their teeth are all similar: simple, pointed, and slightly recurved), but instead consume the entire animal.

Large Red-tails that escape or are allowed to roam a home can be a danger to family pets of all types, especially cats and small dogs. This means that the owner is responsible to keep the snake caged at all times or at least under close observation if it is allowed to "exercise" for a few minutes in the open. Boa Constrictors cannot survive the winter in most of the U.S., though in southern Florida and the Southwest it is not impossible that escapees could make it through the winter. Escapees have ended up in the paper and television headlines when they established themselves under a home or garage and began to feed on neighborhood cats and squirrels.

Prey

Boa Constrictors will eat a variety of warm-blooded prey. Their standard foods in captivity include mice, gerbils, rats, chickens or other birds, and rabbits. The general rule for determining what size food to offer is that prey should be no wider than the girth of the snake at mid-body. Neonates usually will take their first meal shortly after their first shed, usually one to five days after birth. "Pinkies" (newborn mice without hair and their eyes still sealed) are a good food choice for very young snakes since they are both small and nutritious, but within a few weeks most Boas will begin to accept larger mice, at first "fuzzies" (baby mice with fur but eyes not open) and then "hoppers" (mice that have been weaned and are fully active). When the baby Boas are large enough, full-sized mice may be offered. Once the Boa has reached 3 feet, switch to rats, offering one or two every five to seven days. Boas over 6 feet long can eat one to two rabbits every two weeks

Mice are a standard diet for young Boas, while adults prefer rats and rabbits. Many Boas will learn to take frozen, thawed prey.

or three or four large rats. Rabbits are harder to obtain and more expensive than rats, which are stocked by many pet shops.

One of the most important decisions you will need to make is whether to feed live or pre-killed items. Live prey, if not carefully monitored, can injure a snake, possibly causing blindness, gashes, and even death. For the most part, Red-tailed Boas will eat either type, but some may not be willing to take dead items. In this case, live rodents will need to be introduced into the cage. It is very important to remember that live rodents are smarter and more adaptable than any snake. Monitor

the snake's cage closely to make sure the rodent is not harming the snake. Under no circumstances should live prey be allowed to stay in a cage overnight. If the snake does not eat within an hour after the food has been introduced, remove the food and try again in a few days.

Offering pre-killed prey is a humane way to feed your snake. It is easy to purchase frozen mice, rats, and rabbits from pet shops or through mail-order dealers. If using frozen prey, make sure the food is thoroughly thawed and brought up to room temperature before offering; there must be no ice in the body cavity. A Boa can be enticed to strike at frozen prey

FEEDING BOA CONSTRICTORS

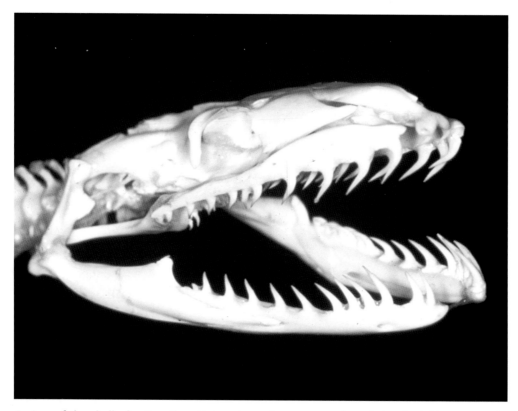

A view of the skull of a Boa Constrictor shows its many teeth and the flexible jaws, modifications for dealing with relatively large prey. Boas are constrictors that kill their prey by suffocation through squeezing.

by holding the rodent with a pair of tongs and gently wriggling it in front of the snake. The snake will strike and usually still try to "kill" the prey, going through the usual constriction motions before swallowing.

If a snake will not eat live or pre-killed rodents, a chicken can be offered. Most Boas will eat chicks even when they show no interest in anything else. Some Boas will even eat chicken that is brought from the grocery store, but this is not advised as various health problems could develop if the meat is even slightly tainted. It is important to make sure the chickens are purchased from a

farmer or breeder and have been properly maintained. There are places that sell chicks frozen only a few days after birth. These can be nutritious and will get a stubborn snake back on a regular feeding regimen.

Feeding Safety

Remember to practice these safety precautions when feeding your snake:

• Look to see where the snake is before opening the cage. If it is too close to the door, use a snake stick or hook to push it back so you can safely place the prey item in the cage. Even the most serene Boas can become nippy if hungry enough.

• Never hold the prey item in your

hand while waiting for the snake to strike. Chances are you will end up with a torn hand. Use forceps (tongs) at the very least.

• Only house one Boa per cage during feedings. Snake owners have been injured more than once while trying to separate two snakes that were fighting over the same piece of food. Furthermore, a pair of angry Boas can damage each other severely.

• When removing a prey item that a snake did not eat, use a snake hook to push the snake away and pull the prey closer to you with tongs. Another method is to use a shield such as a sheet of heavy plastic screwed to a dowel between you and the snake.

FEEDING PROBLEMS

Snakes go through occasional fasting periods, sometimes for valid reasons that simply are inexplicable for the hobbyist. However, there are other times when the fast is not voluntary and can be detrimental to the animal's health. Listed are some considerations that should be investigated.

• Check the air temperature in the Boa's cage. Is it too warm (above 95°F) or too cold (below 80°F)?

• Check the relative humidity, which should be above 70%.

• Has the snake recently been transported? This may cause great amounts of stress. Cover the animal

Because of their smaller head size, young Boas need smaller prey than older specimens. Never harm your pet by trying to see just how large an animal it can force down.

and leave it alone for a few days so it can adjust to its new surroundings.

- Is the enclosure clean?
- Is the snake in the early stages of a shedding cycle?
- Are there any obvious signs of illness?
- Is the snake pregnant? Many gravid snakes lose their appetite during parts of their pregnancy.

Malnutrition is a serious problem for Boa Constrictors. Health problems such as parasites and bacterial infections are precursors to poor eating habits and must be eliminated as soon as possible. Many keepers weigh their adult Boas monthly, keeping a record of the weight and looking for any obvious and continuous loss trends. Weight loss and lethargy are signs of malnutrition, and force-feeding often is the only immediate solution.

The force-feeding process is very delicate and should be done only by an experienced hand. A syringe with soft tubing attached is the most effective tool. A stomach tube where the opening is to the side of the rounded tip often is best. Food should be administered in liquid or semi-liquid form, and the syringe tube worked into the snake's throat, about a quarter to a third of the way down.

A sensible liquid preparation is pureed beef or chicken baby food, mixed with a multivitamin supplement

Recently imported Boas, such as this variety from Corn Island, Nicaragua, may have parasites and be highly stressed, both factors leading to a lack of appetite.

THE GUIDE TO OWNING A RED-TAILED BOA

No matter how much your pet cost, it always needs the best foods fed on a regular schedule. Be careful not to overfeed, and see a veterinarian if you believe it has a problem.

and some water. Remember to keep the water warm (force-fed cold water will shock the daylights out of a snake) and make sure the mixture does not have tube-clogging elements such as suet. Since snakes are stressed by force-feeding, food should be administered in small amounts with rest periods between feedings. Also, a snake that has been force-fed should be left alone for at least 12 hours. Alarming the animal may encourage regurgitation.

Force-feeding is a last resort and should be contemplated only after having a veterinarian check the general health of the Boa. Remember that Boas in nature often undergo long periods without feeding (often several months at a time) but do not suffer any harm. Most keepers greatly overfeed their pets, expecting them to take all their meals regularly and without exception. Missing a few weeks of meals is not really a dangerous situation with larger Boa Constrictors. Force-feeding may actually be more harmful than short periods of fasting and certainly is more stressful.

This striking albino *Boa constrictor constrictor* lacks high contrast between the yellowish white areas and the reddish areas. Other albinos may be much more colorful.

Breeding Boa Constrictors

In the wild in the U.S., snakes usually breed in the spring and eggs are hatched or babies born by late summer to early autumn. Red-tailed Boas, however, are not from the U.S. and follow a different sequence of events, as there are no true seasons in their tropical range.

Snakes that lay eggs, such as pythons, are called oviparous while live-bearing snakes, such as Boa Constrictors, are called ovoviviparous. Boas incubate their eggs internally so that embryonic development occurs inside the female. Embryos are not fed by a placenta but by a yolk sac contained within the birth membrane, which is basically an egg without a shell. When young are born, the babies must then break through the thin membrane that surrounds them.

It is easier to breed live-bearing snakes than those that lay eggs because of the special conditions that must be met in order to incubate the eggs. If it is too cool, too warm, too moist, or too dry, the embryos will perish. The main precaution with ovoviviparous snakes is to not over-handle a gravid female.

SEX DETERMINATION

Most Boa Constrictors become sexually mature by the end of their third year. Age and good body weight are the most important criteria for breeding readiness. The recommended minimum size for a male is 5 feet, and for a female, 6 feet. Captive-bred adults make the best breeders. Imported specimens may take a few years to adapt to captivity before they will breed, although this will depend upon the individual snakes.

Males generally can be differentiated from females by their longer, thicker tails with a relatively slow taper to the tip. Adult female Boa Constrictors have a shorter, thinner tail that tapers more abruptly to the tip. Since Boas belong to one of the most primitive families of snakes, they still have the vestigial remnants of a pelvic girdle and hind limbs that where they project through the skin are called "anal spurs." These are found on either side of the cloaca (vent). Both male and female Boas have anal spurs, but they usually are larger and more pointed in males and more rounded in females. These differences aid the keeper in determining the sex of adult Boa Constrictors, but not of smaller specimens since the spurs in neonates and juveniles are so tiny that the differences are unrecognizable.

The most reliable method of sex determination is to probe the snake with a thin metal rod especially made for the process. A probe that has been lubricated with K-Y jelly or a similar sterile oil is carefully inserted into one of the openings just to the rear edge of the snake's cloaca. If the specimen is a male, the probe can be gently pushed in the direction of the tail to about the level of the eighth subcaudal scale; in a female it can only be pushed to about the second subcaudal scale. This is because the sheaths into which the probe is placed are different in the sexes. In males the sheath houses a long hemipene, half of the deeply divided penis; in females it is a shallow scent gland.

Probe kits usually consist of three different-sized probes and can be obtained through herp-oriented pet shops and through mail-order. Besides being the correct size, the rods should be sterile and well lubricated to avoid injuring the snake. The probing procedure is always somewhat risky and thus should be performed only by an experienced hand.

Some herpetologists determine sex by gently massaging the cloacal area while simultaneously pulling the tail downward. If the snake is a male, this method will slightly expose the hemipenes. This method can be dangerous, however, because irritation and possible bacterial infection to the hemipenes can result. Because of these risks, this technique should be only done by experienced reptile keepers or veterinarians. This method works best on very young snakes whose hemipene muscles are not yet fully developed. In fact, some males are actually born with the hemipenes partially exposed. If noticed, such definite males can be isolated by the breeder and its sex recorded on its card.

PRE-BREEDING COOLING

Breeding cycles are determined by environmental and seasonal changes. Most Boa Constrictors are attuned to

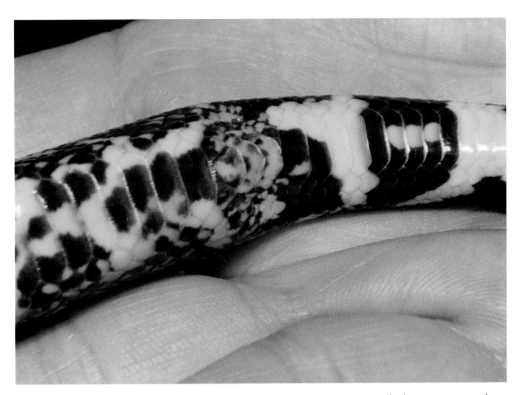

Though probing is the best way of determining sex, an experienced observer can make a good guess at a Boa's sex by looking at the base of the tail and the spurs on each side of the vent.

weather changes associated with wet and dry seasons, it being cooler during the dry season and warmer during the wet. To increase the chances of successful breeding, your goal should be to have animals mate in early spring or late winter months. To allow the snakes to experience a semblance of a natural cycle, you should first mimic the onset of the cooler, drier months. Most breeders time this cooling period (hibernation or brumation) for November or December. This is accomplished by gradually cooling fully mature, healthy Boas over a period of seven to ten days to a temperature that is about ten degrees less than normal. Once proper temperatures have been reached, the cooling should continue for 8 to 12 weeks. (Cooling can begin any time from autumn to the early spring and breeding can still be successful.) Males and females should be separated during the cooling process. On the other hand, some breeders cool several females together with a single male (several males placed together may fight over a female) as breeding can occur during the cooling period.

During the 8 to 12 weeks of hibernation, it is important to maintain day/night temperatures that fall within a narrow range. Daytime temperatures of 80 to 82°F should be maintained for 10 to 12 hours, with a nighttime drop to about 72 to 75°F for the remainder. Thermometers are highly recommended in order to efficiently monitor the temperatures. During this cool period, lightly mist the animals regularly in order to maintain a moderate humidity. Light levels should be reduced during this period as well.

Boas should not be fed during the cooling period and should be closely monitored for any signs of ill health. If a health problem is detected, the snake should be slowly returned to its normal active-season temperature, then given medical attention.

After the 8 to 12 weeks cooling period, gradually over a period of a few days return the Boa to its normal temperature cycle. Humidity can also be increased to normal at this time.

When you are ready to mate the snakes, it is best to place the female into the male's cage since the female is dominant. A male placed in a female's cage often is attacked and could be injured.

MATING

Mating occurs in two stages—courtship and copulation. During courtship, the Boas rub their bodies together and twist and coil about one another. This could be mutual or on the part of one snake trying to attract the other (usually the male trying to entice the female). During this period scents are produced by the snakes that increase their attraction to one another (pheromones). Once both snakes are interested, the male will push his tail under the female's and use his spurs to stimulate her cloacal area. If she is willing to mate, she will submit to copulation by lifting her tail and allowing him to insert one of his hemipenes. The male penis is divided nearly to its base into two segments (the hemipenes) that can be retracted like the fingers of a glove into pouches at the base of the cloaca. The male uses only one hemipene at a time. The hemipene is ornamented with spines and fleshy ridges that help secure it in the cloaca and base of the female oviduct after it swells from fluid pressure, making sperm transfer easier and more certain.

The pair can remain in the mating position for quite some time, and no attempts should be made to separate them during this time. Severe injury could result. After sperm flows into the female's cloaca, it lodges in a thickening at the base of the cloaca and from there flows upward to fertilize the female's eggs. Fertilization may immediately follow mating but more likely will occur a few weeks later.

Leave the snakes alone during the mating process, as some will not mate if they are constantly under observation. You should, however, casually check the pair every now and then to assure that no aggressive behavior is going on, for snakes that are overtly aggressive may indeed harm one another.

Once the initial mating has taken place, the female should be removed from the male's cage to allow her to rest for about two weeks. After the rest period, place her in with another male. If copulation does not occur, there is a good chance she is already gravid.

There is the possibility that Boa Constrictors will not breed every year. It is perfectly normal for a female to breed consistently for a number of years, then skip a year before breeding again. Female snakes also can store sperm for a number of years. Sometimes a female will mate with several males and can utilize their sperm the next year when she ovulates again. The longer she retains sperm, the fewer fertile eggs will be produced during each breeding cycle.

DETERMINING GRAVIDITY

Probably the most difficult part of breeding Boas is determining if the female is gravid. If an increased body girth or softball-sized lumps are observed 30 to 60 days after copulation, it usually signals the presence of mature eggs passing down the

Pregnant female Boas tend to be reclusive and often lose their appetite, and they may become quite aggressive. If you believe your snake is pregnant, it is best to leave her alone as much as possible.

oviducts. Increased girth along with behavioral changes, such as increased or decreased appetite, change in temperament, or increased basking habits, can all be signs of a gravid female. Such signs can also be signs of a health problem, so keep that in mind too.

GESTATION AND BIRTH

When a female is thought to be gravid, good husbandry techniques must be practiced to increase the probability of healthy newborns. Such techniques include the provision of a proper basking site (90 to 95°F), proper cleaning procedures, maintenance of proper environmental conditions, and the avoidance of excessive handling of the snake, as this can cause stillborn babies. Offer food about half the size normally eaten by the snake. Over-feeding a large gravid female could result in damage to the embryos. Don't worry if they won't accept the food, though, as this is normal with gravid snakes.

The gestation period in Boa Constrictors can range from four to ten months, with an average of about six. Many females will continue to feed while gravid, whereas others will stop altogether or, at the very least, eat for the first few weeks of pregnancy and then stop. Many will begin eating again just a few days before giving birth. This is a good indicator that the birthing time is near. Also, a mother will become more active prior to giving birth, and the abdominal

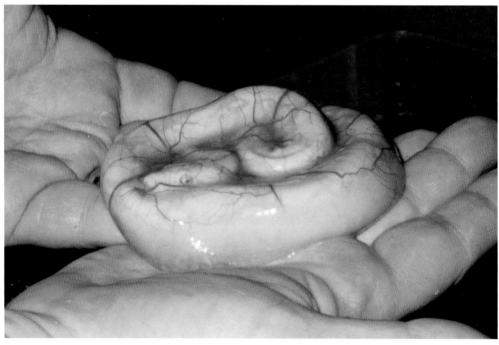

A newborn albino Boa still covered by the birth membranes (sac). The baby will break through the membranes in a few minutes before the sac can dry up and cause a problem.

THE GUIDE TO OWNING A RED-TAILED BOA

Birth in a giant snake can be a bloody business. This is part of a litter of Boas just after birth, including "slugs" or undeveloped eggs. The presence of albinos and normally-colored young indicates at least one parent was not an albino.

mass will move closer toward the cloacal opening.

The birthing process is fairly quick. Contractions push the embryonic sacs containing the fetuses toward the cloaca. Boas usually deliver several fetuses in succession. The neonates will emerge from their embryonic sacs within an hour after birth. If it appears the neonates are having trouble breaking free from the sacs, which may have dried, increase the general humidity in the habitat. Do not hand-assist them at first, for this could, for a number of reasons, kill the baby. Only as a last resort should you open the sac by slitting it for an inch or two with a pair of fine scissors.

Within a few days of birth, the yolk sac contained in the abdomen of the baby will be used up and the umbilical cord will dry up and fall off on its own.

Boas will give birth to anywhere from 11 to 60 young that are between 14 and 20 inches long. Neonates should be placed in their own habitat. Be certain that the environmental conditions are correct. The average temperature of the habitat should be between 82 and 87°F. Hot rocks should never be used with neonates because they do not know enough to get off the rock when it gets too hot and are therefore very susceptible to burns. Under-tank heating pads are preferable heating tools for neonates. A water bowl should have only enough water so that the young Boas can drink but will not drown. Neonates should feed shortly after their first shed, seven to ten days (rarely as much as three weeks) after birth.

Color Variants

Boa Constrictors are very variable animals in nature, showing a variety of differences in background and saddle coloration even within local populations. It is not uncommon for a collection from a limited area to include very dark and very light specimens, some with brown tail markings and others with red. The head pattern can be strong or weak, the saddles connected along the sides or not, and the white spots at the edges of the saddles large or small. Of course there is further variation with geography, from the very dark, speckled Argentine Boas to the very pale, sandy brown Boa Constrictors from desert regions in Peru and even Mexico. Many Emperor Boas from Mexico have very strong head patterns showing a distinct pair of short lines extending over the eyes from the dark line down the center of the head. Because breeders have often mated specimens of Boa Constrictors on the basis of attractiveness of pattern rather than by geography, many of the captive-bred specimens sold today have a highly mixed ancestry.

As more Boas have been bred in captivity, there has been a tendency for more mutations to appear in litters of young. These color variants are genetic and can be reproduced by careful breeding and some knowledge of genetics. Two color mutations are now fairly easy to find, while a third (which may not be purely genetic in nature) also is seen. At the moment these variants are very expensive, but as usual with captive-bred mutations, as the years pass their price is sure to come down.

Albinos

The most striking variant Boa Constrictors are albinos. Contrary to popular knowledge, an albino is not a white animal—it is an animal that lacks dark (brown, black) pigments either because the cells that make these pigments are absent or because they are chemically blocked from producing the pigments. In Boa Constrictors the absence of dark pigments means that yellow and red pigments are accentuated. Most albino Boas show a shadow pattern on the head and body in orange or yellow on a whitish tan background. If the snake has a tendency to red in the tail saddles (a true Red-tail), then the red is extremely bright, pure red without dulling from brown pigments. Some albinos are bright peach and orange with red accents. They have reddish eyes.

Albinism is genetically controlled, so it is possible to breed for albinism if you have a single albino Boa. The trait is recessive, which means that it may be present in the genes but will not show externally if genes for a normal dark pattern also are present. Thus breeding an albino to an albino produces all albinos (recessive X recessive). Breeding an albino with a normal dark Boa produces all dark offspring, but all of them carry the gene for albinism; they are known as hets (for heterozygous) for albinism. If two hets are bred together, albinism reappears in a quarter of the young while half are hets again and another quarter are normal dark snakes without the gene for albinism.

As mentioned, albinism can be caused by different chemical processes affecting the cells that produce dark pigments. Different genes can control these processes, so it is possible to have genetically distinct strains of albinos that when interbred produce normal dark Boas. Virtually all (or perhaps all) albino Boa Constrictors display a similar genetic mutation and will breed true when crossed with each other, but don't be surprised if several distinct strains eventually appear. Certainly there are different intensities of albinism in

Albino snakes are not white, but tend to show increased yellow and pinkish colors. This specimen has nicely developed red saddles on the tail with contrasting yellowish tones.

some lines of albino Boas, some being beautiful animals, others quite mundane.

Hypomelanistic

Another mutation, much more affordable, in Boa Constrictors is hypo (hypomelanistic) Boas. In these animals the colors are subdued and various shades of pale brown, sometimes with very pale heads. The mutation appears to breed true at least within certain strains and is genetic. Some hypo Boas are very pale sandy tan; others have brighter peach tones showing through the brown. Each hypo Boa should be judged individually, but there are some very pretty snakes produced by today's breeders.

Stripes

Many Boa Constrictors show a tendency to join the edges of the saddles on the sides into continuous stripes. This, however, is not what is meant by a striped Boa. In these animals, probably the most striking of the Boa variants, there usually is a broad brown stripe down the center of the back bordered by black. The stripe may be reddish or even bright red and often is broken and not continuous. The red saddles on the tail also may be merged into a single bright red band down the tail.

It long has been uncertain if striping is a genetic variant or one produced by abnormal pregnancies. It has been suggested that if a preg-nant female is kept too dry and cold while gravid, she will produce some striped young. Some breeders, however, claim that the condition is genetic and can be produced within a strain, though at low rates. No matter which explanation is correct, striped Boa Constrictors, especially those showing bright red in the pattern, are uncommon, expensive, and always draw attention.

Red-tails

As you already know, red saddles on the tails of Boas can occur in many different populations and there is no single true "Red-tailed" Boa. Most Red-tails come from humid forests in northern South America, but some populations of even Emperor Boas may have bright red in the tail saddles and some Peruvian populations are noted for brilliant colors. Over the past decade or more, breeders have selectively bred the best available Red-tails in order to constantly increase the brilliance of the colors and the extent of the red on the tail. Today some strains of Red-tails consistently produce young snakes with large bright red tail saddles outlined by bright black and very clean, with little brown duskiness to obscure the colors. Some strains now have the red extending well onto the back saddles as well. At some point, breeders are almost certain to eliminate most of the brown on a Red-tailed Boa

This hypomelanistic Boa Constrictor has the typical subdued but attractive color pattern of the variety, including the pale grayish head. Hypo Boas come in many shades.

and produce a bright red and black patterned snake on a pale tan background, certainly a Boa to be looked for.

Other variants also appear in Boa Constrictors on occasion, but these remain rare. Especially desirable is the leucistic Boa, which really is glossy white (it is not an albino but has a different genetic nature) with blue eyes. Other freak patterns occur, but seldom in numbers large enough to reach the market. No one can predict which mutations will eventually appear in *Boa constrictor* or when, but you can be sure that when a nice pattern occurs, it will eventually reach the market.

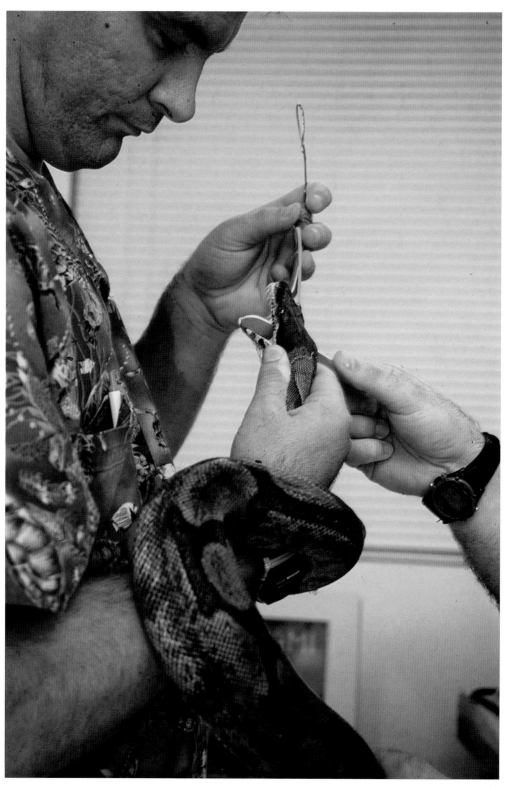

Your veterinarian is your Boa's best friend, next to you. A vet visit after purchase and yearly after that will assure your pet stays healthy and lives a long life.

Illnesses of Boa Constrictors

BOAS ARE HEALTHY SNAKES, BUT...

Captive-bred snakes are less likely to be diseased or stressed than are wild-caught Boas. A wild snake can harbor pests and parasites with little consequence unless the snake becomes stressed, as happens when it is caught and transported to other countries. When snakes are stressed, their resistance to health problems is lowered. Remember, stress can play a huge part in the death of a captive reptile. The same is true with captive-bred animals, although they are, admittedly, a little less susceptible. With any animal, of course, as long as proper husbandry measures are taken, most health problems can be avoided in the first place.

Spread of disease between specimens can be prevented by proper isolation techniques (quarantine). Most snake diseases are not trans-missible to humans, but it is always better to play it safe. Washing hands before and after handling and/or medicating a Boa, and after cleaning an infected habitat, will help prevent the spread of disease to you or other animals in your collection.

An illness in a Boa may show itself in a number of ways. Changes in the Boa's behavior include a refusal to eat, a shift in temperament, changes in basking habits (stops frequenting its favorite sunning or hiding spot), and allowing the upper body to droop while coiled around a tree branch. Visible changes include eyes appearing sunken and body looking emaciated (caved in and bony). Keep in mind that some behavioral changes may occur during a shed cycle.

If you think your snake is sick and you are unsure what to do, don't hesitate to contact your veterinarian. Many illnesses can only be correctly diagnosed and then treated by a vet.

MITES AND TICKS

Mites are very tiny pests that can be found on or under a snake's scales, on the rims of the eyes, and around the vent. They come out from their hiding places in the cage at night to suck blood and can cause a snake to become anemic. They possibly also can transmit some diseases from snake to snake. Snake mites are less than 1 mm (1/25th inch) in length and hard to see, but they can be detected by their silvery droppings, which appear on the snake itself, among other places. At night, they may be spotted as tiny black to reddish dots moving on the body of the snake. They multiply very rapidly and, if left untreated, will diminish a snake's health.

When treating a snake for mites, you must also treat the cage because mites can live in a cage or enclosure without the presence of a snake. Since mites might be able to transmit diseases from one snake to another, the affected snake(s) should be separated and treated in a different enclosure.

To treat mites, place the snake in a covered container with shallow water for three to four hours. While the snake is soaking, remove the contents of the habitat and disinfect all components in a mild bleach/water solution. Discard the substrate, then thoroughly scrub the terrarium with the same bleach/water solution. Put in new substrate, and put back the water bowl and hidebox. Put a small piece (quarter-inch square) of an insecticide-impregnated plastic pest strip into a perforated container and put it at the top of the habitat so that the fumes can circulate and kill the mites. It is important that the Boa does not come into direct contact with the insecticide as it can be as fatal to snakes as it is to the mites, hence the need to put the strip in a container. Remove the snake from the water and dry it before returning it to its enclosure. The ventilation holes in the habitat should be sealed (except for a very small section to permit air circulation) to prevent the mites from escaping.

Other treatments for mites include lightly rubbing down the Boa with olive oil and using various commercial products from the pet shop. Olive oil often works very well, though it sometimes leads to an early shed. Commercial preparations usually work, but they are variable in formulation and often too weak to actually kill mites; if used, be sure to follow instructions exactly.

Ticks are larger than mites and dig in with their mouthparts between a snake's scales. They can be carefully removed with round-edged tweezers or forceps after swabbing the tick

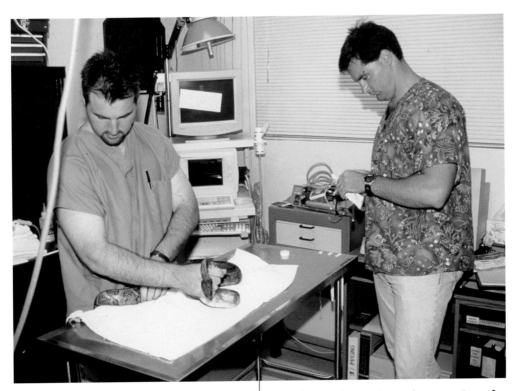

Many ailments of Boas will not yield to home remedies and must have the attention of a veterinarian. Simple antibiotic injections often can cure a dangerous condition in just a few days.

with rubbing alcohol. Alcohol loosens the grip of a tick so it can be more easily pulled off and destroyed. As far as known, the ticks likely to be found on Boa Constrictors (especially common in wild-caught imports) do not carry Lyme disease, but use caution not to get their body fluids on your skin anyway.

Prevention is the best way to avoid the hassle involved with treating mites and ticks. Disinfecting branches, rocks, and driftwood before adding them to a habitat, using a sterile substrate, and isolating new Boas before introducing them into the collection will help accomplish this goal.

MOUTH ROT (Infectious Stomatitis)

Mouth rot is perhaps the most common bacterial disease in snakes. The infection invades the oral region, preventing the mouth from closing completely and making breathing difficult. Mouth rot destroys gums, teeth, and, finally, the rest of the jawbone. Left untreated, death will occur in three to four months. Causes of mouth rot include injuries from striking at the sides of an enclosure or other hard object and rubbing against a screen cover or other surface. In combination with stress, mouth rot will quickly develop into a very serious problem. Poor husbandry techniques such as ignoring

ILLNESSES OF BOA CONSTRICTORS

The swollen jaw may mean this Boa has mouth rot or another oral infection. A trip to the veterinarian is mandatory if you want to prevent your pet from suffering and possibly dying.

dirty habitats and stale water can make a snake more susceptible to mouth rot. Administering vitamin C through prey can decrease the probability of the snake contracting the infection.

When mouth rot is diagnosed, the affected snake should be isolated to prevent the spread of the disease to other specimens; the keeper must be sure to wash hands before and after handling any snake in the collection. This condition is treated by raising the temperature in the affected snake's enclosure to around 88°F. Swabbing the infected area can cause the problem to spread to other tissues in the snake. If the condition is severe, your veterinarian can give antibiotic injections. Since some medications can cause dehydration in snakes, they should be supplemented with an electrolyte solution. If weight loss has occurred, your veterinarian may also recommend vitamin C administered orally to help the Boa build up its defenses. If the disease has progressed far enough for teeth to be lost, they will grow back once the mouth is healthy again. Avoid inflicting further stress upon the animal by excessive handling or forcing it to eat, as this will prolong recovery time.

INTERNAL PARASITES

Parasites are organisms that live in an

animal at the animal's expense. Parasitic infections can go on for years with virtually no problems, or they can progress until the host dies.

Worms are common internal parasites. There are many types of worms that can live in a snake's body. Roundworms, flatworms, tapeworms, and threadworms will cause problems if allowed to exceed levels controllable by the host. Symptoms include refusal of food, regurgitating partially digested food after a few days, and feces that are soft, smell worse than usual, and can be grayish in color. Worms can also be detected by examining the feces to see if the eggs or the worms themselves are present. If you think there is a problem or you have just obtained a wild-caught snake, have the stool checked by a veterinarian to determine if worms are present. Cestodes (tapeworms) grow in the walls of the digestive tract and, along with roundworms, are easily treated. Once the presence of worms has been determined, a broad-spectrum dewormer is generally prescribed.

Certain worms, such as flukes, attack the lungs and are difficult to diagnose. They also are almost impossible to eradicate without harming the snake. The treatment is harsh on the animal and recovery is not guaranteed.

Imported Boas often have mite infections that must be treated immediately. They also will have intestinal parasites that should be monitored and possibly treated by a veterinarian.

Healthy Boas have smooth, often glossy skin without patches of old adherent skin or fungal and bacterial infections. If kept too wet, your Boa probably will suffer from skin infections; if kept too dry, it will not shed properly.

The most serious protozoan infection is amoebiasis. Amoebas feed on materials in the digestive tract. They attack mucous membrane and capillaries in the digestive system, where they enter the blood and spread to other organs. Death will occur in two to four weeks if the disease is not immediately diagnosed and treated in its early stages. Affected snakes will stretch out frequently, drink lots of water, and refuse to eat. Bloody feces may also be observed. Strict quarantine procedures must be practiced to prevent spreading to other animals, and the patient should be brought to a vet as soon as possible.

Salmonellosis is seldom a problem in Boas. The bacteria that cause this disease, a type of food poisoning causing diarrhea in humans, are carried in the gastrointestinal tracts of many reptiles with no adverse effects. It may, however, develop into problems in very old snakes. Signs to watch for are vomiting, refusing to eat, and severe lethargy. Because salmonella bacteria can be transferred to humans and may cause serious problems in children and adults with compromised immune systems, be sure to wash your hands after touching any Boa and also monitor any contact between children and snakes.

GASTROINTESTINAL DISORDERS

Several factors other than illness can contribute to vomiting and regurgitation in snakes. Excessive handling (especially soon after eating), overfeeding, and temperatures that are too low or too high are just a few. Digestion slows down at lower temperatures, but the bacteria living in the snake's digestive tract will continue to work on the food item(s). If the prey spoils in the stomach before the snake digests it, the prey will be regurgitated. Even if proper temperatures are maintained, handling a snake too soon after it has eaten can cause stomach upset and vomiting. After the snake has eaten, it is wise to wait at least 24 hours before handling. If the snake is being properly maintained and regurgitation still occurs repeatedly, antibiotics may be administered, preferably by a veterinarian, since at-home treatments are not recommended.

RESPIRATORY PROBLEMS

Respiratory problems (Upper Respiratory Infections or URIs) often occur in a stressed snake and can be credited to a bacterial or viral infection. Symptoms of URIs include mucous discharge from the nose, bubbly mucus from the mouth, breathing through the mouth because of nasal blockage, holding the upper body erect, whistling sounds from breathing, and the refusal of food. Usually set off by temperatures that are too cold, respiratory infections can be fatal if not quickly remedied. Snakes exhibiting the signs should be maintained at very warm temperatures (around 88°F) and with very low humidity. Even snakes that normally thrive in humid environments should be kept in a dry atmosphere until they have recovered. If the condition persists for longer than a day or so, your veterinarian can prescribe injections or oral antibiotics to administer with an electrolyte solution. Vitamin C injections, as prescribed by your veterinarian, are also helpful.

SKIN PROBLEMS

Skin lesions are often the result of too much humidity or a dirty substrate. If caught early, a skin lesion is easily remedied by thoroughly washing the affected area(s) with a betadine solution then applying an antibiotic cream containing tetracycline. Also, make sure the cause of the problem is eliminated from the habitat. During the recovery period, if the snake has trouble shedding, soak it in warm water and manually help to peel off the shed. Thoroughly dry the snake before returning it to the habitat. If the lesions go untreated, the snake will ultimately die from ensuing infections.

Skin diseases due to fungi (mycosis) are recognized by brown spots that continue to enlarge and usually are found on the ventral scales. As the fungi grow, sores may begin to bleed and show signs of pus. This can spread very quickly to cover the entire snake, so treatment must begin early. Veterinarians can supply the fungicidal agents necessary to eliminate the disease. There are many types of fungi that can cause this condition, so if one medication does not work, be persistent and try another until you find one that does.

Wounds and breaks in the skin can occur when snakes fight, when a prey item bites, or when a snake encounters sharp surfaces in the habitat. Wounds should be treated by bathing the open area in an antiseptic solution. If wounds are deep, they may need to be sutured by a veterinarian.

Burns occur when snakes are in contact with certain heat sources such as heat rocks or exposed light bulbs for too long. Burned areas will be swollen and appear red or gray. Blisters may also be present. In serious cases, scales may be lost. Snakes that have been burned will actively seek shade or cooler areas to help relieve the pain. The snake may twist its body or lie belly-up to try and cool itself. If this behavior, along with the detection of blisters or swelling, is observed, place the snake in lukewarm water to help gradually reduce its body temperature and provide fluids necessary to fight dehydration. The burned skin must be cleansed with water and have an antibacterial ointment applied every day. While the snake is recovering, the habitat temperature should be kept slightly cooler (75 to 80°F) and the area must be kept clean and dry.

SHEDDING PROBLEMS

Ecdysis, or shedding, is a normal process that a snake goes through as it grows when it outgrows its current skin. The normal shedding process is preceded by a darkening and dulling of the skin color (due to accumulation of fluids between the old and new skins) and the eyes appearing cloudy ("blue"), rendering the Boa nearly blind. Activity will be limited, and the snake will usually refuse to eat. This is a vulnerable time for Boas, so they may be aggressive; it is wise not to handle or try to feed them. Provide adequate water for those Boas that like to soak prior to shedding, but be careful not to make the environment too moist or skin lesions may develop.

When a Boa sheds its skin, the snake will rub against a rough surface to begin. Once the first few inches have started, the snake continues to rub against abrasive surfaces until the entire molt has been removed. Providing a rock, stick, or other rough surface will assist the Boa during this time. A successful shed should leave the skin in one piece, but this is not always the case so don't be alarmed if there are a few pieces lying around.

As long as *all* the old skin comes off (especially the caps on the eyes), there is no need for concern. Examine the snake for any pieces that may not have come off during the shedding process.

Possible reasons for improper shedding include dehydration, skin lesions associated with disease or trauma, unclean enclosures, and lack of rough surfaces. In any of these cases, you may need to assist the snake during shedding. Skin from previous sheds, if not removed, can cause a number of problems, including producing a rubber-band-like constriction around the Boa's body.

Improper shedding of the eyecaps, in particular, can leave the snake with limited vision. Removing eyecaps is a very delicate procedure. Using a cotton swab moistened with mineral oil, gently rub along the edges of the eyecap. If the cap will not come off, apply a warm compress and try again. If this does not work, a veterinarian can remove the eyecaps with rounded forceps. Some keepers have found they can remove persistent but loosely attached eyecaps with a small piece of adhesive tape passed over the dry eye.

If the Boa's skin is shed in strips or patches, examine the body for any residual pieces of skin. Left on the snake, these dried areas can cause skin irritation and provide a place for bacterial infections to begin. Soak the Boa in warm water and then try to gently peel away the areas in question. If that doesn't work, again try a little mineral oil. Be warned that if you peel off skin before it is ready to be shed, the snake probably will suffer serious problems including bacterial infections and blisters. Do not be too quick to help a snake with a shed.

Resources

All About Boas

The Living Boas. Jerry G. Walls. T.F.H. Publications. 288 pages.
The best book covering all the boas, not just Boa Constrictors but the entire family Boidae plus its close relatives. Each species is fully described, its range mapped, and its breeding and care discussed. Heavily illustrated.

Big Site

www.kingsnake.com
This gigantic site features something for everyone, with many links plus ads from a very large number of breeders and importers. There are special pages and forums featuring Boa Constrictors as well. Worth investigating.

Emperor Boas

www.strictlyboas.com
This commercial site features only variants of Boa constrictor imperator and is heavily illustrated. It gives a good idea of how variable just one subspecies of Boa can be.

Red-tails

Every Boa Constrictor keeper wants to graduate to Red-tailed Boas. These commercial sites give you an idea of what is available and their cost. Both are heavily illustrated.
www.boastore.com
Features Red-tails from Colombia
www.millerreptiles.com
Includes both Peruvian and Surinam Red-tails

Reptile Vets

www.arav.org
The Association of Reptilian and Amphibian Veterinarians (ARAV) offers membership to veterinarians and vet clinics with strong interests in treating diseases of herps. A membership list organized by state is a good place to start any search for a local vet for your Boa Constrictor

Subspecies

Subspecies of Boa Constrictors never fail to puzzle scientists and keepers, but these two sites at least give an idea of variation in the species and the many named subspecies. Both are heavily illustrated, including links to other sites.
www.boaconstrictors.com/com/com.html
An interesting but rather technical site with lots of breeding information on pure-bred Boas
www.boa-subspecies.com
Includes copies of original descriptions of the subspecies plus many photos of odd variants

Index

Photo Credits

R. D. Babb: 4, 9
M. Bacon: 40
R. D. Bartlett: 7, 8, 10, 11, 14, 21, 25, 37, 38, 39, 49
A. Both: 32
I. Francais: 3, 27, 31, 35, 45
P. Freed: 29, 36
M. Kennedy: 46, 47
E. Loza: 12
W. P. Mara: 19, 56

G. & C. Merker: 1, 51
J. Peelle: 52, 55
K. H. Switak: 13, 17, 22, 58
J. C. Tyson: 57
M. Walls: 43